EYL A

A POETRY COLLECTION

By
Grace Yan

Table of Contents

Part 1: Eye / I

To my parents

You

Went on a
shopping trip with
a large group of friends in
the city and when they walked,
they split like a broken chain,
and you, somehow, the
weakest link snapped
from both ends.
Alone, that's

You

In a maze
as the buildings
full of glass panes stare
at you and you stare back,
thinking how much glass
resembles a human. It's
a master at painting
gray over you,
Stealing

You

and I,
vortexed into
these waves of glass
in this city of steel. Did you
know there's more steel in you
or I than we'll ever know? Did you
know our language curves

waves into walls and
blood into wine?
Do you still
perceive

You?

Harvest

The evening before the child leaves
home for university, she perches
dutifully on the couch's arm at her mother's
insistence for one final maintenance
of her youth: the child
sweeps her mother's graying head for white hair,
repurposed sewing scissors heavy
as a scythe. The abundant silver
that had sparked treasure hunts
now fuels the child's silence.

Her mother once told her that hair whitens
from hardship, stress, ire, that rusted weight
of love. The child carefully cuts
each strand and wonders
which ones feature her—perhaps all
her mother's memory now lies
in her unliving hair, as creases
on a thick paperback book's spine
prove it's been loved.
The child thinks of all the conversations
that never existed—all the arguments
and professions of affection—time herded
into a firing squad row and snips
each possibility away that evening.
She dangles a particularly thick strand
before her mother, who squints her poor eyes
and lies, *Oh, I can see it. It's so white.*

The child worried once if cutting would hurt

4

the hair, but, an adult now, the child
knows better: it's memory that has all the nerve
endings which hurt in a plane of its own
and never grows back. As the failing evening
bathes her mother's now inky head
and the severed silver piling on the end table
a monotonous gold, the child wonders
who she's really reaping.

GRACE YAN

No Title, Not Yet

After "The Hollow Men" by T.S. Eliot.

Reader reads T.S. Eliot's
The Hollow Men
Reader throws down the printed poem and paces
Reader thinks but can't make up their mind
Reader reads the poem again and again
out loud, silent, can't hear them
own voice but recognizes those Hollow Men
overflowing with their own void
Reader hates the void,
the burgeoning black hole
that grows faster
the more attention given
Reader calculates the possibility of walking
out the other side of death's kingdom
a Hollow Man decides the impossibility
decides not to be
if they've got any say in it
and even with none, they still
won't be 'insane' becomes 'fair'
if the alternative is a Hollow stuffed Man
stuck between idea and reality
Reader rereads their copy of T.S. Eliot's
The Hollow Men
and thinks
'The universe went out with a whimper, my *ass*.
Reader nods, laughs, or shouts at the ceiling
the poem themselves.
Reader will not be
Doesn't know what *to* be

not yet.
Doesn't grasp their own vastness
so full brimming bound
to burst, not yet.
Reader doesn't realize they can change the world,
not yet.

Float Test

In the dream, red lotus lanterns float
by the thousands in my grandmother's courtyard.
The lanterns grow roots,
all the rust and soot they shed twining and
burrowing deep into freshwater loam.
Holding hands beneath the surface,
they shine through the fall of dynasties,
riding the cusp of each world turning
on itself over and over.

In the dream, my parents conduct a float test
on themselves: Would they last a journey
across the Pacific? How would a lotus lantern fare
under prolonged exposure to saltwater?
They knew it was safer to practice
a foreign tongue in their homeland
than on the open sea.

In the dream, I am made of ink
condensed lifeblood
120 generations in the making.
My grandmother lifts me
with her brush and paints me
onto a lotus lantern in
thick, unrestrained strokes,
paints me into a prayer,
and sends me bobbing downstream.
There was no float test,
This was the float test.

In the dream, when I land on the shores

of San Francisco, my parents wring
all the saltwater from me,
almost try to raise me in a pond.
I dream I drown anyway,
my nonexistent roots flailing
against a wall called Distance.

When I woke up, I realized I hadn't drowned
but evaporated instead.
I became a wisp.
I became the fog that descends
onto my grandmother's courtyard in the mornings.
I'm sorry I didn't keep
the shape of your brushstrokes.

She nods and smiles.
A prayer is meant to disappear
when it's answered.

2D Me

Suppose this world is origami, and our minds are too
complex and ignorant to comprehend this 2D
existence. Suppose humans are 2D, then
we actually perceive and feel one-
dimensionally.
Look past the illusions and find
reality is just a straight line to follow, from there
to here. But neither here nor there is defined.
No origin, just you—Let me tell you when
a soul is born, it's pressed into a thin sheet
then folded down into a speck of
dust.
That's you.
A point with no definition, confined to a line.

Fold along or around this line the axis
of your being. Or reject this line, and fold
it from the corners. Or let others do
the folding for you if you don't have
the strength to shape yourself.
At least know what you want to be.
And be careful who you let touch you.
You are only allowed one soul to get it
right, get it crisp, and there's nothing crisp
about a soul crushed beneath ten thousand,
frustrated, grubbing hands, pinched and reshaped
until you're more scrap paper than a crane or heart or star
or whatever you decided to be.

Despite the movies, when tumbling down a hill,
you don't roll into a ball.

EYE / I

Your own momentum crushes you. We're all victims
of unwanted creases, rough corners That
stack ruggedly upon
one another
to create clumsy clipped
wings.

It's not necessary to get it right, of course,
or crisp and sharp. Fold yourself into a
failure. It's okay.
Maybe someday, when you unfold
in exploration of other shapes those old creases will help you along.

It's okay if sometimes you wish for the world's edges
to be just a little rounder,
a little thinner.
If you aren't always turning a sharp corner,
then you're crossing
some sort of line,
or traveling on a line,
or waiting in a line,
maybe the grocery line, eyeing the candy bars on the store shelves,
or waiting at an intersection, listening
for an artificial voice to tell you
GO.

Suppose this world is origami and we are just a dot
on an infinite line, then the stars must be dots too
waiting
alongside us.
When you simplify yourself
to a 2D object, hills become plains,
the sky compresses in on you until
you're standing on clouds,

and the world will
unfold to your
desire.

Part 2: Hour / Our

To my reliable mental breakdown besties

Frog

in a dried-up wishing well
spiritless and starved
guard your pennies from the Sun
and teach me
which blue to doubt more:
the Ocean or the Sky

The Fate of Balloons

The clown held the strings together
in his fist, a bird was folding
itself from a thinning line.

The clown looks upon the mass
of huddled sticks, Swallowed
by their clothes, tired from their flight, tired
f losing things, families, limbs, names,
the children were picking at grains of sand.

The natural state of a child:
envision wings on everything
and watch them fly away.
If we attached wings onto those missiles,
will they fly away from us too?

The clown has no answer.
What he does have are balloons,
wingless, full of nothing, fueled by nothing,
but flying all the same.

He wants to tell them:
You can be like these balloons,
fly away on illusory wings,
each feather, a thought, a dream.
You can run away on nothing.

But knows better than to lie:
Even the balloons in his hand
will be shot down once they're freed.

GRACE YAN

"mamihlapinatapai"

(Guinness World Record for most succinct word)

according to the dictionary:

"looking at each other
across the cafe, two strangers
intersect, live asymmetrical
around this point in
the universe's infinite tapestry

hoping that the other will offer
an anchor in a gift-wrapped
promise, a test of revolutions
to follow before the world tilts
sideways once more and forgets
they're there. Each on a mission

to do something of which
neither knows the definition or the destination,
only that this look has—
impossibly— more than one derivative,
to blossom into a rosy curve that

both party's desire
and it can start with
a smile or a surrender
to hope's gnawing, motherly prods,
an infinity-changing course
from a fixed point.
And they know but
they're too strong for this,
believe they can

16

but neither are willing to initiate. "
So, the fixed-point shatters
and two strangers meet
eyes and part, still,
as strangers.

GRACE YAN

The Hoax of Prayer

So, you say it seems the world
has become greener
the hills ablaze
with red wildflowers
shoots snaking into the sun
meeting its gift midway
miracle rains sent
to quell this land's thirst

but mankind must've known
that rains beget storms begets
winds 50 miles an hour
whipping up coasts like
a laughing toddler playing
with a smoothie machine

and mankind must've known
the day we discovered the dead
could power our homes and vehicles
there would be a day we run out
of the living or a day we fill
those empty graves with something else

and mankind must've known
when Prometheus gifted us fire
there came a cost we couldn't choose
and isn't it funny how history is only
one story cycling through different
bends of the same river
becoming smoother and rounder
until we're nothing but a grain of sand

until we're not even anything
when the green creeps on—a miracle!
remember a thirsty land—saved!
remember the sender—amen!
remember what was borrowed
must one day be returned.

GRACE YAN

Legs of the Empire

A tribute to my grandfather

Creatures with four legs lived better than him
who carried the mountains he climbed
with him down the mines because the mountains
too, have nowhere else to go after the terraforming.
The pores of his skin choked tight with black
dust; he picks through silver alongside two-legged
wretches he never bothered to know the names of.
He tunnels blood veins and nerve vessels a mile
beneath scarred, lifeless skin.

This is how an empire is born,
chiseled into life by the pickaxe of a wretch,
no more significant than an ant.
Watch his thigh muscles contract and pump with a dull sheen,
mind dwelling on the meager porridge from that morning,
simply water with a rice-like haze when
farm dogs are fed at least scrap meat and bone.
But he continues, sapient enough, suffering enough
to understand the minerals mined today
will feed his future grandchildren.
This generation, with a diet of metal scraps
will live and die on the construction
beams of their unfinished homes.

This is how an empire learns to walk
because we were all infantile animals once.

Dear Antique Store Owner

I wonder what price you sold that
Sakura hairpin for? The one you sold
to an East Asian mother-daughter pair
that looked like sisters, except
one was a fading poem of youth
written on a skull-colored scroll
and the other was spilled blood
over spilled ink, still a poem but
unreadable, foreign.
Do you remember?

I wonder why you bought that used candle
for ten dollars
it was an old soy candle
except half the wax was gone and
who's going to keep using that?

I wonder why you've got furniture in
your shop, not chairs or bedside lamps I'm talking
1700s couches and even older dinner tables,
the bulkiest furniture possible, and they
might as well be from the Stone Age, what—
You think some fossils live here and
need furnishing?

I wonder why your windows are always
shut and shades pulled down. Is there something
so good about the air in this musky,
a ramshackle place worth confining?

I wonder if you will live to see the day

stargazing becomes reckoned a lost
art. Did you know we can barely see any
anymore? Jealous of city lights and phone
screens that devour all the pairs of eyes
we have to offer,
they turned away from our world.

                                        Stars—

if you can find any,
shouldn't you be selling them too?

Dear Antique Store Owner
whose name I never bothered to ask; I wonder
why you became an antique
store owner in the first place.
Are you just a hoarder or
lonely?
Is there anything
you love?

Monk: a Documentary

see, monk
it's about time for a career change:
you and your old tripod on pilgrimage
through a desert, searching
for sanctuary:
no dawn: yes,
blinding flash over
a dune that wasn't there yesterday

remember the dawn over dune:
now, obsolete, instead
capture it
kill it, dissect it, name it:
morning: no
mantra: no
Man: yes, it has always been Man: it's true,
monk, you should still remember

how to shoot: yes,
mount the machine, focus the lens
adjust the exposure, focus, aim:
pull the trigger:
ka-cha!

there, you got it, monk:
truth, distilled into a bullet,
body bags in a memory chip
tucked into
an album on a garage shelf
or a famed, framed wall photo:
nameless child: headless parent:

even the headlines agree:
you've done a good job

see:
how long does it take to master
truth: it's everywhere, so long as you know
where to probe, collect ripe
tear trails: there's enough life-soaked
into this desert
to feed you for decades.
see: you can make a new career out of this
see: what this new career makes

Part 3: Deer / Dear

To all the poems I never finished

The Actor

The actor knows he has failed
when he leaves the theater
and doesn't know whether to be
the bumbling sidekick with a goose grin,
the shadowy figure lingering in
the alleyway, the jolly gentleman
with a cowlick, impeccable
with every inflection,
the boy-convict hungry and motherless,
the invincible hero
who only makes new mistakes,
the disguised king
leaving violets at his lover's door,
the fortune teller haunted
to insanity by those he swindled, or—
the most harrowing option of all—
to not decide altogether and to live
as his own ghost.

Fragments of God

My grandma searched for
fragments of God on riverbanks,
waded through shallow waters as
tadpoles swam around her ankles.

She was a quiet woman,
lived the way of nature, the way
of listening and finding poetry
in magnificent piles of sand,
the decay of fallen trees,
and the young shoots covering them.

Once, she showed me her collection
of what she called "God's tears."
A palmful of tiny rocks picked off the river floor,
rocks, not minerals, not gems–
rocks, gypsum, pyrite, shale,
other jagged, moss-covered, unidentified stones,
glittering in the afternoon sun.

Now, grandma is 78,
walks with a cane,
lives alone,
can't remember my name.
But she remembers her rocks.

Each time I visit, I take a bamboo box
from my grandma's closet,
show her the gypsum, pyrite, shale
and she picks them up with trembling hands
as if she were holding

the greatest treasures on Earth.
We are only fragments, unqualified
to judge the beauty of other fragments—
the way those rocks tumble down from the mountainside,
the way they were once boulders, and will,
in the future, be little grains of fine sand–

Somewhere on the other side of the world,
a piece of sandstone breaks
away from the cliff
and falls into the sea,
a stray cat finds a companion,
an ant finds a fallen cracker on cement.

Grandma's rocks wait
for the day they return
to a river to be
made whole.

That for which we find words

After Friedrich Nietzsche

The sunset haunts the study. Enclosed,
a pen-holding corpse furtively Writes
a manuscript with a deadline long past.

From deep beneath the corpse's words, a hand
rooted in dulled spite reaches– it flails, then grasps.
Death hauls itself through the paper barrier.

The corpse laughs, "Finally found the strength?"
To which Death responds with a cold, careful kiss
on the corpse's cheek.

Death's gaze falls on the barefaced liquor bottles
strewn in every corner of the room,
empty caskets of counterfeit peace.

Death stares, and the corpse feels a judgment
so limpid its hand slacks, and the pen falls,
sinking into the table. Death asks

Why fake what you restlessly deny? The corpse
beholds the strewn papers and, knowing it's just a dream,
screams, "I must finish! I will go with you after, but…"

…It, too, knows its last sentence, lone and unknown,
unfinished on the page is the end: "That for which
we find words is—" The corpse looks up. Death

stretches a hand: a greeting, a peace offering,
or both. Taking it, the corpse stills. The sun falls.
At last, rested deep beneath, it finds itself:

"—something already dead in our hearts."

"That for which we find words is something already dead in our
hearts" is a quote from Friedrich Nietzsche.

My Deer

My English teacher once said
Everyone gets one dead deer poem—
This is my second.

I thought I was ready for the first,
but something went wrong when
my deer was born ugly and stayed ugly
even in death.
Where are my promised twin swans?
Sacred transformation? White-tailed corpse?

Maybe it was my fault. Maybe
it was the deer. Maybe
I'm just jealous of the other
deer created from a mere sigh,
springing into the arms
of their creators, slaughtered
in a graceful, procedural ritual.

Maybe it was the way my deer
said to me, "You have no right to grieve."
Or maybe it was shame.
I buried my deer hastily
beneath six feet of similarly ugly prose.

I wonder why I tried creating a deer in the first place
when so many could be found beneath me.
We live on a planetary graveyard:
corpses of humans who housed giants,
of empires once thought eternal,
of trees with language

rooted deep and fossilized,
waiting in the earth—
of imaginary deer, the philosopher's favorite

toy, a chimerical figment of Death
an up-close, scythe-less form to study.
Age after age, we return, designing
different hypotheses,
different scenarios
to kill the deer in a way that matters,
to pull its soul back to the living
again and again.
Unbreakable until broken.

A poet, I—
desperate for my own genius, I—
turn to the place of thieves:
Standing before this graveyard,
a sea of corpses reflecting stars
so realistic I don't know
which side of the world I stand on,
my pen becomes
a shovel.
I dig.

Sorry, I'm here to steal some dead deer.

I hit my first body the same way
a black hole announces itself, a tickling
warp in light. A deer lies before me,
not as a deer but as a vision, a question.
It's big enough for a pyre but small
enough to steal without being missed.
I light the match.

I pick up a handful of grays, chalky,
unclaimed truth. I wonder
if I sprinkle this ash into the dirt,
will something natural grow?
If something blossoms,
will a bird unfurl from its petals?
Featherless fledgling covered in soot,
as ugly as it will be beautiful—
Is this the deer I stole?

Made in the USA
Las Vegas, NV
12 December 2024

13943688R00022